No Lex 12-13

Weekly Reader Books presents

S.O.S

Skills On
Studying

HELP IS ON
THE WAY
FOR:

Taking Notes

Written by Marilyn Berry
Pictures by Bartholomew

Living Skills Press
Sebastopol, California

Executive Producer: Joy Berry
Editors: Nancy Cochran, Susan Motycka and Kate Dickey
Consultants: Kathleen McBride, Maureen Dryden and Donna Fisher
Design: Abigail Johnston
Typesetting: Curt Chelin

For a complete catalog of other living skills materials,
write to: Institute of Living Skills
P.O. Box 1461, Fallbrook, CA 92028

So you need to start **taking notes**.

Hang on! Help is on the way!

If you have a hard time knowing how to take notes

- from a textbook,
- in class, and
- for special projects...

...you are not alone!

Just in case you're wondering...

...why don't we start at the beginning?

What Is Notetaking?

A **note** is a brief record of acts or ideas.
When you take notes, you are writing down
important information.

A note is also a reminder of information you have read or heard. You are expected to remember a large amount of information every day. If you learn to take notes, you will be able to recall a lot more of that information.

Why Is Taking Notes Important?

Learning to take notes can help you in everyday life. Here are two examples:

- Taking notes helps you remember important dates.

- Taking notes helps you remember thoughts and ideas.

Learning to take notes can help you in school.
Here are two examples:

• Taking notes helps you study for tests.

• Taking notes helps you gather information for
school projects.

The older you get and the more you go to school, the more you will find that taking notes is an important skill. Notetaking becomes easier with practice. But first you need to learn about the best methods for taking notes.

Writing Notes to Yourself

There are many important details that you need
to remember during a school day. You do not
need to memorize them all. Learn to write notes
to yourself as a reminder. Here are some
examples:

Lists of "Things to Do"
Keep a page in your notebook of "Things to
Do." When there is a task that you need to do,
write it down on your list. As you complete each
task, cross it off your list.

Assignment Book

Keep a special notebook, just for assignments. As each assignment in class is given, write it in this notebook. Be sure to include this information:

- the subject
- the due date
- books and materials needed
- details of the assignment
- a sample problem, if possible

Keeping an assignment book will help you remember your homework.

Idea File

When you think of a creative idea, write it down so you don't forget it. You might not need the idea at that moment, but it could come in handy later. Keep a file of ideas for such assignments as

- written reports,
- creative writing,
- special projects, and
- art work.

Taking Notes for School

The hardest part of taking notes is deciding what to write down. The key is to pick out the most important facts and ideas and to leave out the information that is not important. But sometimes it is hard to decide what is important and what is not.

There are two basic rules that can help you decide if a piece of information is important or not. Remember these rules as you take notes.

RULE ONE

The information is important and should be included in your notes if it
- helps you answer a question about the topic you are studying, or
- helps you understand the topic more clearly.

RULE TWO.

The information is *not* important and does not need to be included in your notes if it

- repeats something that has already been said about the topic you are studying, or
- does not help you understand the topic more clearly.

USING YOUR OWN STYLE

Everyone develops his or her own style of taking notes. As you continue to take notes, you will develop your own style, too. Here are some ideas:
- Use either whole sentences or short phrases.
- Learn how to shorten words that are used often. For example, use "trans" for transportation.
- Use initials for names that are used often.
- Learn to be brief but not so brief you can't understand your own notes.

DAILY SCHOOLWORK

There will be times as you do your daily schoolwork when taking notes will be very helpful.
Taking notes helps you
- keep track of the information you are expected
  to learn,
- pick out the information you don't understand
  so you can ask questions,
- be prepared for class, and
- study for tests.

Keeping a Notebook

It's a lot easier to take notes and keep track of them if you use a notebook. You can have a separate notebook for each of your school subjects. Or, you might want to keep all your notes in one binder with a section for each subject. No matter which of these methods you choose, it is important that you

- have a notebook available for taking notes, and
- know where to find your notes when you need them.

Taking Notes from a Textbook

When your teacher gives you a reading assignment in a textbook, you will learn more if you take notes as you read. Try following these five simple steps.

Step one: Look over the assignment.
- Read the title and the introduction.
- Read any phrases or words in bold type.
- Look at the illustrations and their captions.
- Read the conclusion.

Step two: Ask questions.
- Look at the questions at the end of each chapter. They will tell you what important information to look for as you read.
- Or, write down several of your own questions that came to mind as you looked over the assignment.

Step three: Read the assignment.
- As you read, think about your questions.
- When you come to some information that answers a question or seems important, carefully mark the place with a paper clip. (Remember the two rules of notetaking.)

Step four: Answer the questions.
- After you have read the assignment, close your book and try to answer all of the questions.
- Write down the answers in the proper section of your notebook.

Step five: Check your answers.
- Check your answers to make sure they are right and correct any mistakes.
- Check each place you marked to make sure you wrote down all the important information.
  Be sure to remove all your markers.
- Save your notes and study them for future tests.

Taking Notes in Class

Throughout the day, your teacher explains a lot of important information to your class. It would help you remember this information if you wrote down some notes. Taking notes in class is easy if you are prepared and know how to do it.

Be Prepared
- Always have your notebook and a sharpened pencil ready.
- Make sure you can hear the teacher clearly.
- Make sure you can see the chalkboard.

How to Take Notes in Class

1. Turn to the proper section in your notebook. Write the date and the topic at the top of a clean page.
2. Listen and watch for clues of important points such as:
   - "Today we're going to discuss..."
   - "This is important..."
   - "Please remember this..."
   - A point that is repeated several times
   - Anything written on the chalkboard
3. Write down only important facts and ideas.
4. Ask questions when you do not understand something.

Copy Your Notes

Many times when you take notes in class, you need to write down the information quickly. Your notes might be messy and disorganized. If so, copy your notes onto a clean piece of paper at the end of the day. This will help you

- review the information that was discussed,
- sort out any information you don't understand (be sure to have your teacher explain these items), and
- organize your notes for future studying.

SPECIAL RESEARCH PROJECTS

There will be times in school when your teacher will assign special projects that require some research. For these projects, you will be gathering a lot of information from several different resources. To help you keep it all straight, you will need to study a system of notetaking and follow it carefully.

There are three notetaking systems which you can use when gathering information for a project. You can use

- note cards,
- topic sheets, or
- a note chart.

Each system works in a different way. You might want to try each one once to see which system works best for you.

Note Cards

The use of note cards is a popular system of notetaking. As you do your research, you simply write down any information you need on 3" x 5" or 4" x 6" index cards. Once you have gathered all the information for your project, the cards can then be easily arranged and rearranged into any order you choose.

When using note cards for your research, there are some important rules to follow:
- Write only on one side of the card.
- Identify your resource on every card (such as the title and author of a book).
- Write down the location of the information (such as a page number).
- Put only one complete fact, idea, or quote on each card. Try to limit the information to one or two sentences.
- Number the main points of your project. Then assign the information on each card to one of your main points. Write the number of the main point at the top of the note card.

Bibliography Cards
As you gather information for your project,
it is important that you keep track of the
resources you use. Each resource should be
recorded on a separate card called a bibliography
card. This information will come in handy when
you need to
• look up information a second time,
• check a quotation, or
• prepare a bibliography (a list of the resources
  you used for your project).

The information that you record on a
bibliography card should include the same
information you will need for your actual
bibliography. If you use the proper form
on your note cards, you will be able to copy
the information right onto the bibliography
page of your project. Here are the proper forms
to use for three types of resources:

BOOK

Frost, Brian. The U.S. Presidents. San Fran.
Parkside Press, 1985

MAGAZINE

MacDonald, Garrett. Who Was Grover Cleveland?
Historical News, July 29, 1985 pp. 8-16.

INTERVIEW

Interview with Grover Cleveland V. Sebastopol,
Cal March 6, 1985.

Topic Sheets

Using topic sheets is another good system of notetaking. Instead of using index cards, you write down any information you want to use on labeled sheets of paper. Each sheet of paper is labeled with one of the major points or topics of your project. All topic sheets are kept in a special notebook.

8½"×11" LOOSE LEAF NOTEBOOK

NOTE BOOK DIVIDERS

LINED NOTEBOOK PAPER

RULER

PEN OR PENCIL

Making Your Topic Sheets
To set up the topic sheet system for your project you will need
- an 8½'' x 11'' loose-leaf notebook,
- notebook dividers (one for each topic),
- several pages of lined notebook paper,
- a ruler, and
- a pen or pencil.

Instructions:
- Decide on the main points of your project and put them in a logical order.
- Write one main point on each of the notebook dividers and put them in the notebook.
- Draw a two-inch margin on the left side of three pieces of notebook paper.
- Write "Resources" above the left margin on each page.
- Write the title of the first point at the topic of each page and put them in your notebook.
- Make up topic sheets for each section of your notebook.

Using Your Topic Sheets

As you research your project, keep your notebook handy. When you find some information you can use, record it in your notebook.

- Determine which main point the information falls under.
- Turn to a topic sheet in that section of the notebook.
- In the left hand margin, identify the resource (such as the title, author and page number of a book).
- Write down the information you need on the topic sheet.
- Leave a space between notes.
- Use only one side of the page.

Bibliography Sheets

You will need to keep track of your resources, just as you would for the note card system. Write "Bibliography" on a separate sheet of paper and keep it in the back of your notebook. As you use a resource, record all the information you will need for the actual bibliography page of your project. Remember to use proper form.

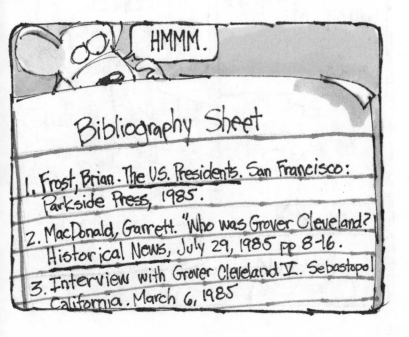

HMMM.

Bibliography Sheet

1. Frost, Brian. The U.S. Presidents. San Francisco: Parkside Press, 1985.

2. MacDonald, Garrett. "Who was Grover Cleveland?" Historical News, July 29, 1985 pp 8-16.

3. Interview with Grover Cleveland V. Sebastopol, California. March 6, 1985

Note Chart

A note chart is not as portable as note cards or topic sheets. However, a note chart displays your whole project at once. This allows you to get an overview of the project as it progresses.

Making Your Note Chart
To set up the note chart system for your project you will need
- a piece of poster board (or a large piece of paper approximately 22'' x 28'',
- a yardstick, and
- a black marking pen.

Instructions:
- Decide on the main points of your project and put them in a logical order.
- Using the yardstick and marking pen, divide the poster board into columns. There should be one column for resources and one for each main point of your report.
- At the top of the left hand column, write "resources."
- At the top of each remaining column, write one of the main points of your project.
- In each of the "main point" columns, make boxes large enough to write at least one or two sentences.

Resources	Early Years	White House Years	Later Years

A REAL **WORK OF ART.**

Using Your Note Chart

As you research your project, fill in your note chart with the information you want to use.

- When you use a resource, list it in the resource column of your chart. Be sure to include all the information you will need for the bibliography page of your project.
- When you find information you can use, determine which main point the information falls under.
- Write down the information in the proper column next to the resource in which you found it.

Resources	Early Years	White House Years	Later Years
MacDonald Garrett "Who Was Grover Cleveland? Historical News July 29, 1985 pp. 8-16	Born Mar. 18, 1837	Democrat Served 2 terms	Died June 24 1908

TAKING NOTES
FROM WRITTEN RESOURCES

When you find a written resource that has information you can use, try following these easy steps.

1. Look in the table of contents and the index to find the sections related to your topic.
2. Read one section through. As you find useful information, mark the place with a paper clip.
3. Go through the section a second time. Think about the main points of your project.
4. If you can use the information, summarize it in your own words on your note card, topic sheet, or note chart.
5. Do this with each section of the resource.

TAKING NOTES AT AN INTERVIEW

When you are using an interview as a resource, try these suggestions:

1. Get organized ahead of time.
   - Have plenty of paper and sharpened pencils ready.
   - Make up a list of questions that you need answered.
2. Listen carefully and take careful notes.
3. Make sure all your questions are answered before you leave.
4. Thank the person and credit him or her in your report.

No matter which notetaking system you choose or what types of resources you use, there are some basic rules you should follow.

- Always try to write clearly.
- Study one resource at a time and go over your notes before moving on to another resource.
- Be brief. Try to limit each note to one or two sentences.
- Take notes only on information that is related to your topic.
- Copy quotes exactly including punctuation.
- Except for quotes, write down information in your own words. This lets you know that you understand the information. It also saves you from having to rewrite the information later.
- If your notes don't agree, check a third source.

WARNING!

If you learn the notetaking skills in this book, your schoolwork will become easier, and...

...you will probably become a better student!

THE END

About the Author

Marilyn Berry has a master's degree in education with a specialization in reading. She is on staff as a producer and creator of supplementary materials at the Institute of Living Skills. Marilyn is a published author of books and composer of music for children. She is the mother of two sons, John and Brent.

Weekly Reader Books presents

Skills On Studying

HELP IS ON
THE WAY
FOR:

Using
Resource
Materials

Written by Marilyn Berry
Pictures by Bartholomew

Living Skills Press
Sebastopol, California

Weekly Reader Books offers several exciting
card and activity programs. For information,
write to WEEKLY READER BOOKS, P.O. Box 16636,
Columbus, Ohio 43216.

Executive Producer: Joy Berry
Editors: Nancy Cochran, Susan Motycka and Kate Dickey
Consultants: Kathleen McBride, Maureen Dryden and Donna Fisher
Design: Abigail Johnston
Typesetting: Curt Chelin

For a complete catalog of other living skills materials,
write to: Institute of Living Skills
P.O. Box 1461, Fallbrook, CA 92028

Weekly Reader Books edition published by
arrangement with Living Skills Press.

So you need some information and you don't know how to get it!

Hang on! Help is on the way!

If you are having a hard time

- choosing your resources,
- knowing where to go for your resources, and
- knowing how to use your resources...

...you are not alone!

Just in case you're wondering...

...why don't we start at the beginning?

What Are Resources?

A resource is anything that supplies information.
Here are some examples of resources:
- a person, such as an expert on a subject,
- a place, such as a museum or a place of business, and
- materials, such as books, films, or tapes.

Why Are Resources Important?

Resources Help You in Everyday Life

There will be times when you will need information to accomplish a task or just to satisfy your curiosity. Knowing how to use different types of resources helps you to find information on your own without having to depend on others.

Resources Help You in School

There will be many times in school when your teacher will assign schoolwork that requires the use of outside resources. Knowing how to find and use the proper resources will save you time and effort.

No matter what information you may want or need to find, there are many different resources that can help you. The key to unlock this world of knowledge is to learn
- how to choose your resources,
- where to go for your resources, and
- how to use your resources.

Choosing Your Resources

When you are given an assignment that requires some research, you will probably find there are more resources available than you need. Since you cannot use all of the resources available, you will want to choose the best ones for your assignment. Choosing your resources is easier when you
• understand the assignment, and
• understand your topic.

Understand the Assignment

To help you choose the best resources, you need to make sure you understand what the teacher expects from you. Ask questions about the assignment and write down the information. Here are some questions you may want to ask:

- When is the assignment due? (This will tell you how long you have to gather information.)
- How long is the assignment?
- What kind of information is required? (General or detailed information?)
- How many resources are required?
- Are there types of resources you can or cannot use?

Understand Your Topic

Before you choose your resources, you will need to have a general idea of what information you are looking for. Write down questions about your topic that you want to answer. Be as specific as possible. If you do not know anything about your topic, you may need to get some background information before you make your list of questions.

Make Your Choices

Here are some guidelines to keep in mind as you choose your resources:

- Choose resources that clearly answer your questions.
- Choose resources that are reliable.
- Choose written resources that are at your reading level.
- Choose resources that you find interesting.
- Be creative. Try to use different types of resources.
- Try to use the most current resources about your topic.

Materials As Resources

There are two major types of materials that are available to you as resources: written materials and audio-visual materials.

WRITTEN MATERIALS

Written materials are the most popular resource for most students. They include:

Reference Books

Reference books are materials that are *not* meant to be read from cover to cover. Instead they are designed to give you specific information quickly and easily. You will find a guide at the front of most reference books that will teach you how to use the book. If you begin by taking a few minutes to look over this information, it will save you time in the long run.

There are so many different reference books that most libraries do not have room for them all. It would be worth your while to take some time and see which reference books are available in your library. Here are some of the more popular reference books that can be found in most libraries:

- encyclopedias
- dictionaries
- biographical dictionaries
- almanacs
- atlases

• Encyclopedias

Encyclopedias are one of the most popular types of reference books. They are simple to use and easy to understand. There are two different types of encyclopedias:

1. *General encyclopedias* provide basic information on many topics in many different subject areas.

2. *Subject encyclopedias* provide more specific information on topics in one major subject area.

When you cannot find the information you need in a general encyclopedia, check to see if there is a subject encyclopedia you can use.

When To Use an Encyclopedia

Encyclopedias are most useful when you need
- a quick overview of a subject,
- background material about your topic,
- an idea for an outline on your topic,
- to verify a fact (such as a name, date, or place), or
- to answer a simple question.

Encyclopedias are a good starting point for your research, but they should *not* be your only resource.

How To Use an Encyclopedia

There are two simple ways to find your topic in an encyclopedia:

1. The information in an encyclopedia is arranged in alphabetical order by subject. The letters included in each volume are printed on the spines of the books. Look up your topic in the appropriate volume. If your topic is listed, you will either find information on the topic or a cross reference that will refer you to another volume.

2. Most encyclopedias have an index that will help you find your topic and other related information. The index is also arranged alphabetically by subject. When you look up your topic in the index it will be followed by
   • the subject under which you will find your topic,
   • a letter that tells you which volume to use, and
   • a page number that tells you where to find your topic.

YOUR TOPIC

THE SUBJECT UNDER WHICH YOU WILL FIND YOUR TOPIC

Siamese kite
   Kite *picture* C - 2 15
Siamese Twins
   Twins [Identical Twins] T: 435
Sian [China]
   Han Dynasty

VOLUME LETTER

PAGE NUMBER

• Dictionaries

Most people think that dictionaries are useful only when you need to know the meaning of a word. However, there are many different dictionaries that provide all kinds of information. Here are just a few:

- the general word dictionary
- dictionaries that give the history of words
- dictionaries of slang words
- dictionaries of synonyms and antonyms
- foreign language dictionaries

The *general word dictionary* is an important resource that can provide you with a variety of quick information. You can use it to look up

- proper spelling of words
- abbreviations
- pronunciation of words
- parts of speech
- other forms of a word
- different meanings of a word
- histories of words

How To Use A Word Dictionary
The words in a dictionary are listed in
alphabetical order. By using the guide words at
the top of the pages, you can locate a word
quickly and easily. Once you find a word you will
also find a wealth of information (To understand
the abbreviations used in a dictionary, remember
to check the guide in the front of the book.)

• Biographical Dictionaries

A common assignment in school is to gather information about a famous person. A good resource for this type of assignment is a biographical dictionary. These books contain brief articles about peoples' lives. The articles in most biographical dictionaries are arranged alphabetically according to the persons' last names.

• Almanacs

An almanac is a collection of facts and other interesting bits of information. These books are usually published every year and include current information from the previous year. The topics covered are listed in an index in alphabetical order. For current facts in a variety of areas, the almanac is a good resource.

• Atlases

An atlas is a collection of maps that provides information about different places around the world. Atlases are especially valuable for research in the area of geography. The information included in an atlas is listed in an index in alphabetical order.

Nonfiction Books

A nonfiction book is another type of written material that can be a valuable resource. The information in a nonfiction book is usually centered around one major subject. There are nonfiction books written about almost any subject you can imagine.

Locating a Nonfiction Book

Nonfiction books are located together in a special section of the library. You will find them listed alphabetically by subject, title and author in the card catalog (or microfiche). Here's how to locate the books you need:

- Look up your topic in the catalog.
- Choose the books that are most closely related to your topic.
- Carefully copy down the call numbers, author and title.
- Find the call numbers on the nonfiction shelves.

How To Use Nonfiction Books

How you use a nonfiction book depends on the information you need. You may find a book that follows the outline of your topic exactly. In that case you might want to read the whole book. Other books may have only a chapter or a page on your topic. In that case you will want to read only those sections.

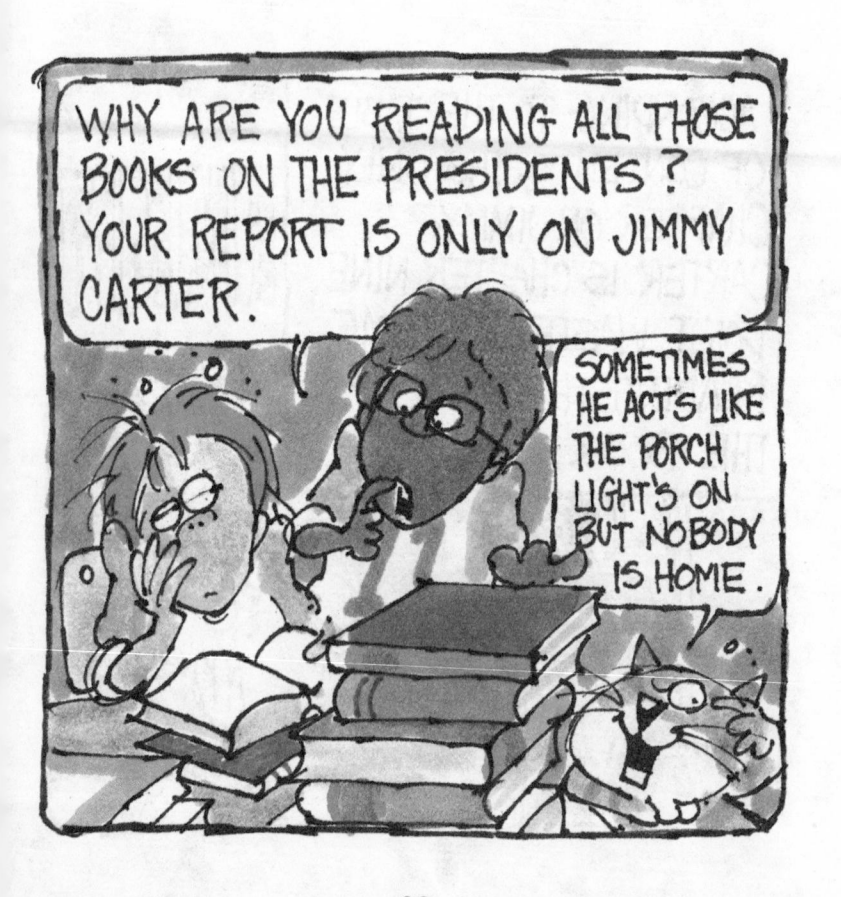

There are two tricks you can use to find out if a nonfiction book has the information you need.

- **Check the table of contents.** The table of contents is the list of chapter titles in the front of the book. If you read through the titles, you can get a general idea of what topics are covered in the book.

- **Check the index.** The index of a nonfiction book is located in the back of the book. It is more specific than the table of contents. The index lists all the information that is included in the book. If your topic is not listed in the index of a book, it probably does not have the information you need.

Periodicals

Another type of written materials that you will want to consider are periodicals. Periodicals are resources such as magazines and newspapers that are especially valuable when you need current information.

The Reader's Guide To Periodical Literature is an index that lists the articles printed in over 150 magazines. The articles are listed alphabetically by author or subject. Here is an example of an entry:

SUBJECT ENTRY

NAME OF ARTICLE

AUTHOR

BASKETBALL

Rising to New Heights.   Jim Ratt

il Sports News 9:34-36 F '85

ILLUSTRATED

NAME OF MAGAZINE

VOLUME NUMBER

PAGES

DATE OF ISSUE

FEBRUARY 1985

How To Use the Reader's Guide
To find the most current information on your
topic, start with the most recent volumes. You
can then work your way back through earlier
volumes until you find the information you need.

• Look up your topic.
• When you find the articles you want to read,
  write down this information for each one:

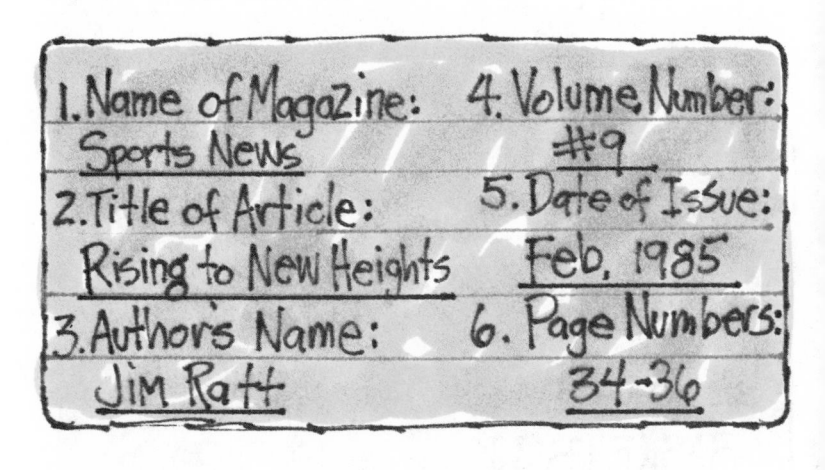

1. Name of Magazine: 4. Volume Number:
   Sports News   #9
2. Title of Article: 5. Date of Issue:
   Rising to New Heights   Feb, 1985
3. Author's Name: 6. Page Numbers:
   Jim Ratt   34-36

• Your library will have a list of the magazines it
  subscribes to. Check this list to see if the
  magazines you want are available.
• Go to the magazine area in your library and
  look for the issues you need.

The first few times you use *The Reader's Guide*,
you may want to ask your librarian for help.

Newspapers

Newspapers are an especially valuable resource
when you need information about
- a very recent event, or
- the events that took place on a specific date.

You can locate this information by contacting a
newspaper office directly or by using your library.
Every library subscribes to different newspapers
and uses different methods for storing them. Your
librarian can tell you which newspapers are on file
at your library and how to locate the information
you need.

I WANT TO FIND WHAT OTHER EXCITING THINGS HAPPENED THE DAY I WAS BORN.

LET'S FIND A NEWSPAPER THAT WAS PRINTED ON YOUR BIRTHDAY.

The Vertical File

Your library has a special filing cabinet called the vertical file. A variety of pamphlets and other materials that are hard to store are kept in the vertical file. These materials are arranged by subject and include a wide range of information. Be sure to look over the material in your library's vertical file. You never know what you might find.

AUDIO-VISUAL MATERIALS

You do not have to limit your research to written materials. You can add variety and interest to your assignments by using audio-visual materials. Check the card catalog in your library to see if any audio-visual materials are available on your topic. Look for records, tapes, films, and filmstrips. Also, check your television listings for educational television programs. You might get lucky.

People As Resources

Talking directly to people can be an exciting way to gather information. Here are some advantages to using people as resources:

- You can get current information that hasn't been printed yet.
- You can get special information that can't be found anywhere else.
- You can get your questions answered without having to sort through information you can't use.
- You may find it more interesting to discuss your topic with an expert than to just read about it in a book.

PERSONAL INTERVIEWS

There are many people in your community who can offer you valuable information on many different topics. Most libraries have a community resource file that lists these individuals. If there is someone in your community who is an expert on your topic, try to arrange a personal interview with that person.

- Call ahead and make an appointment.
- Explain who you are.
- Explain why you need the information and how it will be used.
- Give the person your topic and two or three general questions to consider.

Once your interview is arranged, spend some time preparing for the meeting.
- Do some background research on your topic so you will be able to ask intelligent questions.
- Find out about the person you are interviewing. In what way is he or she an expert on your topic?
- Make a list of specific questions you want answered.

To make the best of your time and the interview, follow these guidelines:
- Be on time.
- Listen carefully.
- Take careful notes *or* record the interview (if you use a tape recorder, be sure to ask permission first).
- Make sure all your questions are answered.
- Ask for suggestions about other resources on your topic.
- Thank the person and credit him or her in your report.

PERSONAL SURVEYS

It can be fun to do your own research by conducting a personal survey. A survey is gathering information by asking several people the same questions. Here are some guidelines for a successful survey:

• Make sure a survey is appropriate for your topic.
• Limit the number of questions.
• Try to use questions that require a simple yes or no
• Include as many people as you can.
• Be fair when you summarize the results.

Places as Resources

There are many places in your community where you can find information on a variety of topics. Some of these places include:

- museums
- historical societies
- specialty libraries
- places of business
- community service organizations

Some of the places in your community may offer free tours and literature. To take advantage of these tours
- call ahead and make an appointment,
- make a list of questions you need answered,
- be on time,
- take notes during the tour, and
- collect any literature available.

You can keep your research fun and exciting if you follow two simple rules:
1. Be creative. When it's your decision, choose topics that interest you. Always look for unusual information that will make your assignment unique.
2. Stay away from resources that are too difficult for you. Stick with resources that are interesting and easy to understand.

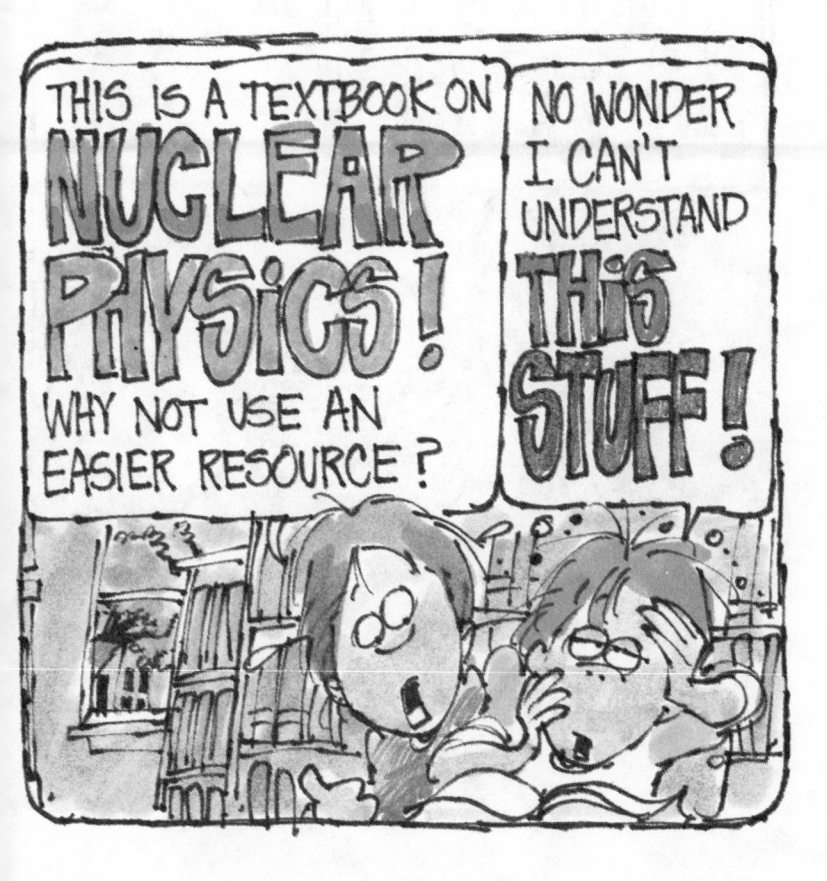

WARNING!

If you learn how to use your resources, you will probably become a better student, and . . .

. . . there's no limit to what you might learn.

THE END

About the Author

Marilyn Berry has a master's degree in education with a specialization in reading. She is on staff as a producer and creator of supplementary materials at the Institute of Living Skills. Marilyn is a published author of books and composer of music for children. She is the mother of two sons, John and Brent.